Leaving Microsoft to Change the World

JOHN WOOD

Level 3

Retold by Chris Rice

Series Editors: Andy Hopkins and Jocelyn Potter

Pearson Education Limited
Edinburgh Gate, Harlow,
Essex CM20 2JE, England
and Associated Companies throughout the world.

ISBN: 978-1-4082-3171-5

This edition first published by Pearson Education Ltd 2011

5 7 9 10 8 6 4

Set in 11/14pt Bembo
Printed in China
SWTC/04

Penguin Books Ltd a Penguin Random House Company

Acknowledgements
The publisher would like to thank the following for their kind permission
to reproduce their photographs:

Alamy Images: Geoff Marshall 3; **Room to Read:** vi, 9, 16, 21, 27, 35, 38, 39, 44, 47
Cover images: *Front:* **Room to Read**

All other images © Pearson Education

Every effort has been made to trace the copyright holders and we apologise in advance
for any unintentional omissions. We would be pleased to insert the appropriate
acknowledgement in any subsequent edition of this publication.

For a complete list of the titles available in the Penguin Readers series please go to
www.penguinreaders.com. Alternatively, write to your local Pearson Longman office
or to: Penguin Readers Marketing Department, Pearson Education,
Edinburgh Gate, Harlow, Essex CM20 2JE, England.

Contents

Introduction

*I wanted to help, but I couldn't think how. The head teacher seemed
to read my thoughts. His next sentence changed my life forever.
"Maybe, sir, one day you will come back with books."*

In 1998, John Wood was a busy, successful man, working
in an important, well-paid job for Microsoft in Australia.
Then one day, during a three-week vacation in Nepal (his
longest vacation for nine years), he visited a school in a small
Himalayan village. That visit changed his life. There were
seventy children in each classroom, no desks, and an almost
empty library cupboard. With the help of his father in the
United States and Dinesh Shrestha in Nepal, John returned
to the school with eight yaks and hundreds of books. But that
was only the beginning of the story. John decided to help more
than one school in Nepal. He wanted to help the world!

With nothing more than his business skills and the hope of
giving children around the world a better future, John Wood
started the charity Room to Read. In this book, you can read
John's wonderful, almost unbelievable, story.

John Wood was educated at the University of Colorado and
Northwestern University in the United States. He worked
for Microsoft from 1991 to 1999. During this time, he ran
important parts of Microsoft's international business, working
in Australia and China. In 1999, at the age of 35, he left
Microsoft and began to work full time for Room to Read.
When he is not working, he enjoys tennis, running, reading,
winter sports and good red wine. His home is in San Francisco.

John Wood opening a new library in Nepal

Chapter 1 "I Promise You, We Will Meet Again."

There was an icy wind from the mountains as the sun went down behind the snow-topped Himalayas. A young Nepali boy offered me a drink.

"Do you have a beer?" I asked.

"Yes!" he replied happily. He ran off to get it.

Today was the first of a twenty-one-day vacation walking in the Himalayas. It was 1998, and the start of my longest vacation in nine years—a welcome break from my job as a sales director at Microsoft's busy office in Sydney, Australia. I had three weeks without e-mail, phone calls, and heavy city traffic; three weeks of walking three hundred kilometers around the mountains with a big, heavy bag on my back. On day ten, I hoped to reach a height of almost 6,000 meters—the highest that I have ever climbed in my life.

The Nepali boy returned with my bottle of beer.

"I'm sorry, sir, it's not very cold," he said. But then he had an idea. "I'll be back in three minutes," he smiled, and he ran down to the river.

As I waited for him, he put the bottle into the icy water. Then he smiled and waved.

A middle-aged Nepali man at the next table laughed at the boy's simple, intelligent way of solving the problem.

"Who needs a refrigerator?" I asked, as a way to start conversation with him. "Are all the children in Nepal as smart as this?"

"The people up here are good at solving difficult problems in simple ways," he replied. "They have so little. For example, dinner is cooked over a wood fire because they don't have ovens."

The boy returned with a very cold beer—and a big smile on his face.

1

Pasupathi (the man at the next table) soon started to tell me about his work in Nepal. There were seventeen schools in this area. His job was to find the necessary equipment for them. This was very difficult because most of the schools were far away from the main road, along narrow, hilly paths.

"Are Nepalese children good learners?" I asked him.

"Here in the country areas we have many smart children," he replied. "They want to learn, but we don't have enough schools or equipment. Everyone is poor so there isn't much money for education. In this village we have a primary school but the nearest secondary school is two hours' walk away. Also, many children stop their education too early. Their parents need them to work on their farms."

As Pasupathi poured himself tea, he told me more.

"Some days I am very sad for my country. I want the children to get a good education, but it isn't happening. About 70% of Nepalis can't read. They aren't stupid. They want to learn, but the government doesn't have enough money for schools, teachers, and books."

Our conversation interested me very much. I could learn about the real Nepal, and not only the Nepal that tourists see.

"Where are you going tomorrow?" I asked him.

"I'm going to visit a school in the village of Bahundanda," he replied. "It's a three-hour walk up steep hills."

I was excited. "Can I go with you?" I asked him.

"Of course," he smiled. "I will be proud to show you our school."

The next morning, after breakfast, Pasupathi and I began our trip into the hills. After two hours of hard walking and an hour's steep climb, I followed him into the village. Children in dark blue pants and light blue shirts ran past us toward the school, ready for the start of the school day, waving at the amusing foreigner with the big heavy bag on his back.

The village of Bahundanda, Nepal

Pasupathi introduced me to the head teacher and I was shown around the school. There were eight classrooms with seventy children in each. The floor was hard earth, and the sun on the metal roof made the rooms as hot as ovens. There were no desks, and the children crowded together on long, wooden seats with notebooks on their knees.

The head teacher next took us to the library. A sign outside the door proudly said SCHOOL LIBRARY, but inside, the room was empty except for a ten-year-old map of the world on one wall.

"This is a beautiful library room," I said. "Thank you for showing it to me. I have only one question. Where are your books?"

The head teacher took out some keys and opened a cupboard. Inside the cupboard there were very few books.

"How many students are there at the school?" I asked him.

"We have 450," the head teacher replied. Then, noticing the

look of shock on my face, he added, "Yes, this is a very big problem. We want our students to enjoy reading, but that is impossible."

I wanted to help, but I couldn't think how. The head teacher seemed to read my thoughts. His next sentence changed my life forever.

"Maybe, sir, one day you will come back with books."

After a long, interesting talk with all the teachers at the school, I stood up to leave. The English teacher shook my hand.

"Please sir, when you come back with books, you will be very welcome," he smiled.

I imagined my return to the school, with a yak and hundreds of books on its back. I suddenly felt very excited.

"I promise you, we will meet again," I said.

I have always loved books. When I was a child, in the United States, my mother read me stories at bedtime. When I was older, I borrowed twelve books a week from our small, local library. I couldn't stop reading. On long car trips, or late at night when everybody was asleep, my nose was always in a book. I couldn't imagine a world without books for children. That is why I was so excited. I really wanted to start a library for the children in Bahundanda.

Three weeks later, I went to an Internet café in Kathmandu and sent an urgent e-mail to more than a hundred people in my address book.

From: John Wood
Subject: Books for Nepal—Please Help
Dear Friends,

Nepal is one of the world's most beautiful countries. It is also one of the poorest. While I was on vacation in the Nepal Himalayas, I was invited to visit a local school. There were 450 students but only about twenty books in the library. I need your help! I promised to return with enough books for a good school library. If you'd like to help, you can do one of three things:

—Send books for young students who are learning English to my address in Australia or my parents' address in the U.S.

—Send this e-mail to other people that you know.

—Send me money so I can buy more books.

Please do something to help these children. Ask your friends! Thank you.

John

On my final morning in Nepal, I felt sad about leaving. I loved the country with all my heart. *But I'm going to return,* I thought. *I'm going to come back with hundreds of books and find a yak!*

Chapter 2   Return to Bahundanda

Back in Australia, my thoughts quickly moved away from Himalayan libraries, back to the busy world of computers. I had an important job to do for Microsoft. I was working hard on business plans until late every evening.

One night, while I was working, I received an e-mail from my father.

Subject: You need to get home soon!

Dear John,

I am writing to invite you to visit us in Colorado. Your project for books for Nepal has been more successful than you thought! I think that we have about 3,000 books here.

Can you come and help me look through them? I don't know what the schools need. We also have to decide how to ship the books to Nepal.

Love,

Dad/Woody

Six weeks later, I made the twenty-five-hour trip from Sydney to Colorado. While I was flying across the Pacific, I read a thick international report on education. I learned that 850

5

million people in the world were unable to read. Of those 850 million, about two-thirds were women. I also read that over 100 million children of primary-school age didn't go to school.

I felt shocked and angry. *Something must be done now!* I thought. *If nothing is done immediately, it will be too late for all these poor children.*

I thought hard about this problem. I was trying to help one school in Nepal. But that wasn't enough. Why couldn't I do more? A hundred years ago a very rich man, Andrew Carnegie, used his money to open 2,000 libraries across North America. Could I do the same for the people of Nepal and other poor countries? Parents around the world all had the same dream. They wanted their children to have a better life. I wasn't as rich as Carnegie, but I was young. Carnegie was an old man when he started building libraries. I wasn't going to wait until I was an old man. I wanted to help now!

When I arrived in Colorado, I immediately started to look through the books in my father's garage. It took me two days. My father and I put them in boxes for their 8,000-mile trip to Nepal. But then I thought of a new problem. How could we get the books to Bahundanda? The school was a two-day walk from the nearest road. We couldn't just put them in the mail.

At dinner that night, my father suggested an answer to this problem. He belonged to the Lions Club in Colorado, and this club had members all around the world.

"Maybe members in Nepal will work with us," he said.

He was right. He checked on the computer, and found information about the Lions Club in Kathmandu. From his downstairs office, he sent them an e-mail describing our project.

The next morning, he had a reply:

Dear Mr. Wood,

We received today your request for help in sending books to a school in Bahundanda. We would be happy to help you in your project. When you are ready to send the books, please tell me. One of our club members works in the government. He will be able to help get the books into the country.

Because you have so many books, can I make a suggestion? Maybe you can donate books to more than one school. All of our schools here have the same problem—few books.

Thanking you from Nepal,
Dinesh Shrestha

After this success, my seventy-three-year-old father was even more excited about the project. He wanted to help me take the books to Bahundanda and other schools in the Himalayas. But I didn't want him to come with me.

"Travel is difficult in Nepal," I told him. "There's no television, no meat, no clean bathrooms or comfortable beds."

"That's no problem," he said, amused at my excuses. "I fought in World War 2. I'm stronger than you think."

But I didn't want him to come for other, more private, reasons. I thought that he was too old for a long trip like this. I also often found it difficult to talk to him. And now he wanted us to spend two weeks together in the Himalayas.

"I'll think about it, Dad," I said. "I'm not sure when we can go. We don't have to decide immediately."

Three days later, I was back in Sydney, working hard again on business plans for Microsoft. One evening, I received an e-mail from my father:

Dear John,

Today I mailed thirty-seven boxes of books to Nepal. The total cost was $685. Please send me a check when you can.

I hope you're very proud of your project. It's going to help a lot of children.

Why can't I go with you to Nepal?

Love,
Dad

Suddenly feeling very emotional, I read the e-mail again.

I'm so selfish and stupid, I thought. *My father has worked hard on this project, too. Why don't I want him with me in Nepal?*

I sent an immediate reply.

Dear Dad,

I'm sending you a check for $3,685—$685 for mailing the boxes of books, and $3,000 for a ticket to Kathmandu. We can go in March or April, after the books have arrived. See you in Nepal!

Love,

John

♦

I pulled my woolen hat down tighter and enjoyed the smell of wood and smoke from the small fire in front of me. I was back in Nepal after almost a year, and I felt good. The quietness of the Himalayan morning was very different from the noise and dirty air of Beijing.

I was now living in Beijing, and I was a business director for Microsoft in China. I was excited by my new job, but there were already problems with life in Beijing. The city was very cold and there was no space in the city for running or cycling, and I had a bad cough from the unclean air.

But this morning in Nepal I felt good. After breakfast, my father and I continued to climb up the narrow path to Bahundanda. We were followed by eight yaks, each one with a big box of books on its back, and their driver.

The sun was hot as we climbed the steep path. The yaks were a long way behind us, so I stopped at a small river. As I was washing my face, someone sat next to me. I looked up and saw a young Nepalese man. He was drinking from the icy water.

"*Namaste,*" he greeted me with a very friendly smile.

"*Kasto Cha,*" I replied. ("How are you?")

"Today, sir, I am very happy. Today is a very big day for our village. A man is coming today with books for our school. We

John with books for Bahundanda

do not know how many, and we do not know his nationality. I think he is from Holland. Our students are waiting. I am going there now to greet his arrival."

I felt at the same time very proud and very surprised. *Is our project really so important to the people here?* I thought. I shook his hand and told him my name. Then I introduced him to my father.

"We're from America," I said. "The books are a short way behind us. Can you show us to the school?"

"My name is Sushil," the young man replied with a smile. "I'll be happy to be your guide."

As we got close to the school, I heard the sound of children laughing. I walked more quickly, and minutes later I was in the village. The head teacher smiled happily at me like an old friend and took me in his arms. Then he invited me to walk to the school between two long lines of students.

The first student in the line, a five-year-old girl with long black hair and a bright smile, hung orange flowers around my neck. Other children laughed and ran toward me. They all wanted to hang flowers around my neck!

My father and I moved slowly along the line. Finally, covered in flowers, we reached the school. We were taken up onto a small stage, and there we were greeted by all the teachers. The children went quiet, and the head teacher made a short speech:

"This is a very big day for our school and our village," he said. "We now have a library full of books. Inside books, you will discover the hidden mysteries of the world. With books, you can learn, and you can make a better future for your families and for our country. We want to thank Mr. John and his father for this beautiful gift. We promise always to be careful with the books."

After the speech, the children crowded around noisily as we opened the boxes. We gave them all books, and they looked, wide-eyed with excitement, at color photos of animals, stars, and strange people in foreign lands.

As we watched, a teacher joined us. He took my hand in his. His large, brown eyes shone with happiness.

"You have given our children so much," he smiled. "And we have so little to offer in return."

I felt very emotional. Words were hard to find. My heart was filled with a strange but beautiful new feeling. For these children, there was more hope today than there was yesterday. All of this was because of a simple request a year ago—"Maybe, sir, one day you will come back with books." My father and I were very serious about that request, and we worked hard. But the real success was the donations from my friends around the world. They sent me books, and these children's happiness was only possible because of them.

Chapter 3   Walking Away

Two days after our trip to Bahundanda, my father and I were back in Kathmandu. On our first day there, I woke very early and walked the quiet streets alone. I was thinking about the happiness of the children in Bahundanda. But I was also thinking about the millions of children in other villages who still had no books. I wanted to help them, too, but how?

As I walked the streets, I thought hard about the problem. There was no easy answer. I now had a new job with Microsoft in China. I was very lucky because I earned a lot of money. I also had an excellent future, a beautiful girlfriend, an expensive car, a full-time driver, and free travel around the world. Everything was going right.

But a little voice inside me was saying something different: *Does it matter how many copies of Microsoft Windows are sold this month? There are millions of children in the world without any books. Almost 70% of children in Nepal will never learn to read! Lots of people want to work for Microsoft. But how many people want to build schools and libraries in Nepal? Nobody is doing that job.*

The sun was now high in the clear blue sky, and the streets were filling with people. Suddenly, my mind seemed clear. *Maybe there is life after Microsoft*, I laughed to myself. *And maybe that life will be here in Nepal. I must follow my dream. I know I'm going to be poorer. But I'm going to be a lot happier, too.*

I felt good about my new future plans, but I was worried, too. *This big change in my life isn't going to be easy,* I thought. *A lot of people are going to be angry with me. And what do I know about life outside a big, internationally successful company?*

Later, on the four-hour flight to Beijing, I thought about my two biggest problems: Sophie and Michael.

Sophie was my girlfriend, and she also ran the China office of a big international company. She was beautiful and intelligent.

11

She could speak perfect French, Spanish, Czech, and Mandarin Chinese before she was thirty-three! We were in love but, sadly, we had very different interests. Unlike me, she wasn't interested in walking up mountains. She was more interested in expensive hotels, large pay checks, and beautiful clothes.

Michael was my boss in China and, more than anyone, I helped him with his busy working day. But he was more than a boss—he was also my friend. We often met after work for a meal or a game of tennis.

Sophie and Michael are both going to be very unhappy about my news, I thought. I felt terrible about that.

Twenty minutes after leaving Beijing Airport, I arrived at our big, expensive apartment. Sophie was waiting for me. There was the smell of my favorite Mexican food in the kitchen, and a bottle of my favorite Australian wine in her hand. As we drank a glass of wine, I told her about my trip—our visits to the schools, and the look of happiness on the children's faces. But Sophie was more interested in other things.

"How did you wash without hot water?" she wanted to know. "How was the food cooked without electricity?"

"Cold showers and wood fires," I told her.

She gave a small, weak smile.

Then I decided to tell her about my new plans.

"I want to go back to Nepal quite often," I said.

"But I want our next vacation to be on a beach in Thailand," she replied.

"I'm not talking about vacations. I'm thinking about leaving Microsoft completely."

She looked shocked. "How can you?" she said. "We've just arrived, and you've got an important job. One day you'll be Microsoft's top man in China."

"Those things don't seem important to me any more. I have to follow my heart."

"But how are we going to live? Microsoft pays for this apartment. We won't have enough money …"

"We can move to a smaller apartment. I don't know. I haven't really thought about it yet."

We sat down to a very quiet dinner.

♦

For the next few weeks I was very busy. Bill Gates, the head of Microsoft, was coming to China. It was my job to organize his visit. I decided not to tell Michael yet about my plans to leave Microsoft.

Even after Bill Gates went home, I didn't tell Michael immediately. I was still worried about giving up my job. *Can I really live without a regular pay check?* I asked myself repeatedly. *I can live carefully from my savings, but only for about five years.* But each time, a small voice inside my head gave me the same answer: *Why do you want money in the bank if you can't spend it on your dreams?*

I discussed the problem with my father. "Why am I more excited about a donation of books for children in Nepal than by the success of Windows in China?" I asked him.

"Different things have become important to you now," he said. "Maybe it's time to stop working for other people. Maybe it's time to be your own boss."

On a beautiful May morning in Beijing, I arrived at the Microsoft building. I nervously made myself a cup of tea, and went straight to Michael's office. I decided to tell him the news quickly.

"I'm sorry, Mike, but I can't work here any more," I said. "I don't like this city and I don't like my life. Different things have become important to me."

He tried to say something, but I didn't listen.

"I know you got me this job in China. I'm very grateful.

13

But I'm sorry, Mike, I have to go."

He looked shocked, and I felt terrible.

"You're my most important guy here," he said angrily. "I need you here. Nobody can do the job as well as you."

"I'm too emotional to talk about it now," I replied. "But I'm not going to change my mind. We can discuss my leaving date later in the week."

With those words, I hurried out of his office. I decided not to go straight home. I had a meeting in Hong Kong, and I drove straight to the airport. I needed time before I spoke to Sophie.

Two days later, back in Beijing, I told her about my meeting with Michael. I loved her very much and I didn't want to hurt her. But I had to be completely honest with her.

"I have to go," I told her. "I'm leaving everything behind me—my job, the city, our home, even you ..."

Sophie couldn't believe her ears. Angrily, she took down a painting from the wall. It showed a seat under a tree. It was our favorite painting because we always imagined ourselves there, in that quiet place, after the end of our working lives. She threw the painting at the wall. That night, I moved into another bedroom. Six weeks later, I was flying out of Beijing. I watched the city below me, covered in its usual cloud of dirty gray smoke. As the city became smaller, I sat back with a big smile on my face. For the first time in months, I felt calm, happy, and free.

Chapter 4   A New Life

In December 1999, my project became a real charity with a name: Books for Nepal. I was excited, but a little worried, too. I knew nothing about charity work. I had no idea what to do next. An old college friend, Jim, helped me. He explained how to organize the charity correctly. He and his wife, Jen, also donated $10,000.

Many books were coming in from ordinary people and large companies. More than one hundred Nepali schools wanted to be part of our library program. But books weren't our only project. We were also starting to build schools.

Dinesh, in Nepal, worked as a volunteer, but he wanted a few young Nepalese guys to work full-time on our projects.

"We can employ local college graduates for $200 a month," he told me.

Jim and Jen's money was enough for a team in Nepal, but my new organization needed a lot more money.

Not every possible donor was as friendly and helpful as Jim and Jen. Many people refused to help me during the first months of the project. But this didn't worry me too much. My experience at Microsoft taught me one very important lesson. If nobody refuses you, you aren't asking enough people.

Sometimes I did feel very unhappy. I asked an American Himalayan organization in San Francisco for help, but they showed no interest in my project. After that meeting, I sat for a long time in a coffee shop, watching the crowds of busy people on the sidewalk outside the window. This was a new experience for me. At Microsoft, everybody returned my phone calls. Many people helped me with my projects and I had lots of money. Now I was alone. I felt small and useless. I had big dreams but, with no experience in the world of international charity work, I didn't know the right people. *Maybe I've made a big mistake*, I was thinking.

Suddenly, I received an e-mail. It was from Dinesh. He was working hard, as usual. It was 2 A.M. his time. The subject line made me happier: "Good news from Nepal."

Dear John,

Here are some photos of two of our new schools. As you can see, the parents are helping to build them. The head teachers of the two schools would like you to visit this fall. Can you come?

Minutes earlier, I was losing all hope in my project. Now my heart was filled with happiness. The future looked bright again. I immediately sent the photos of the projects to friends. Maybe they knew people who would like to help? Next, I e-mailed a travel company for information about flights to Nepal.

A few weeks later, I went to the San Francisco offices of DRF. This was a fund that belonged to a successful company. The owners of the business, Bill Draper and Robin Richards Donahue, wanted to help fund small, young charities. They were offering $100,000 a year for three years to the organizations that they liked.

I felt nervous as I walked into their 29th-floor offices with beautiful views of the Golden Gate Bridge. I was interviewed by Jenny, the fund director. She was friendly and interested in my project. But then she gave me bad news:

"I like your organization, but you've already done a lot.

One of the first Room to Read schools in Nepal, paid for by John

16

We're more interested in projects that are just starting."

"But, but, but ... we're still very small," I said, worried about failing again.

"I don't know. You already have a few schools and libraries in Nepal. You're talking about moving into other countries."

"Yes, we have two schools and twelve libraries," I agreed. "But without funds, we can't do any more. We have big plans, but we need more money."

She said nothing, so I continued talking. Finally, she said, "I'll discuss your project with other people. Then I'll tell you what we decide."

I walked out of the office without much hope of success.

Two weeks later, the telephone rang. "Hi, John. This is Rhonda from Bill Draper's office. Bill heard from Jenny about your work. He would like to come to your office and meet you tomorrow. He'll need about three hours to discuss your business plan."

This was excellent news—but my business plan was in my head, on my computer, in e-mails from Dinesh ... I had less than twenty-four hours to bring it all together! I worked in my office until 2 A.M. I slept on the floor until 6 A.M., and then worked on the plan for another seven hours.

At two o'clock the next afternoon, Bill and Jenny arrived at my small office. I gave them two copies of a thirty-five page business plan that was still warm from the printer.

Bill Draper, a large, healthy, seventy-year-old man with silver hair, wanted to know all about me and my plans for Books for Nepal.

"Tell me first about your people," he said. "If your people are not right, there's no hope for your organization. You say that groups of people are going to help you. Who are they? Give me names."

"A lot of people want to change the world," I replied. "But not many of them are able to leave their jobs. I understand this.

17

My goal is for anyone—from rich bankers to ordinary school teachers—to help us. After work or on weekends, these volunteers can organize meetings and parties for possible donors. For example, at a party here in San Francisco last fall, a team of volunteers made $35,000 for the project. That doesn't seem like very much, I know. But it's enough to build four schools in Nepal. Our organization also works with local donors in Nepal to build the schools, libraries, and computer rooms. With their help, we also fund scholarships for girls. So local people are giving time and money, too."

"Excellent," Bill smiled. "I like people working together like this. It's a better way of helping than free gifts from outsiders."

We talked about my business plan for a few more hours. Finally, Bill stood up and shook my hand.

"I will enjoy working with you," he said. "I want people who aren't afraid of hard work."

Two weeks later, I heard that DRF were giving us $100,000 a year. It was a large amount, and I was very excited. But I also knew that this wasn't the end to our fund-raising work. It was only the beginning. A charity should never work with only one donor. We needed more.

Chapter 5   A Young Man Named Vu

In 2001, with the success of our programs in Nepal, I began to think about Books for Nepal in a second country. Vietnam interested me for many reasons. It was a poor country, almost destroyed by past wars. Many ordinary people only earned $1 a day. They believed that, with education, their children could earn $2 or $3. But the main reason for my new idea was a young man named Vu.

In 1996, I went on a two-day business trip to Hanoi. While I was hurrying to meetings, I noticed other foreign visitors with bags on their backs. *They're lucky*, I thought. *They're seeing the country slowly, in their own time.* Of course, I was lucky, too, because Microsoft was paying for my visit. But was I really experiencing the country?

A year later, I went back to Vietnam for a two-week vacation. With a bag full of books and an empty notebook, I planned to travel from the south (Ho Chi Minh City) up through the long, thin country to the north.

My days in Vietnam were quiet. Every morning, I wrote down my thoughts in my notebook over a strong, hot cup of Vietnamese coffee. In Hue, on the fourth day, a Vietnamese boy of about seventeen years old came up to my table. He had short black hair and a soft, kind face. He was wearing blue pants, a clean white shirt, and plastic shoes.

"My name is Nguyen Thai Vu," he said. "But call me Vu. That's easier."

"Nice to meet you, Vu," I replied. "Please, sit down. My name's John. I'm from America."

"Good, because I want to practice my English with you. Is that all right?"

"Of course. But how much practice do you really need? Your English seems perfect to me."

"Oh, no, it is not so good," he said. "This is a small hotel, so there are not many guests. I do not have as much practice as I would like."

"You work here?"

"Yes, but maybe you haven't seen me because I work at night. I see in the guest book that you will be here for three days. So maybe you will be my friend and every morning we can practice my English."

I wanted to help, but I didn't like the idea of regular meetings on vacation. I quickly changed the subject and pointed to an old book in his hand, *Learning Microsoft Excel*.

"Are you studying computers?" I asked him.

"Oh, yes, I study computers as much as I can. Computers are important for Vietnam's future."

"I work for Microsoft, Vu. As part of my job, I sell Microsoft Excel."

"Really?" he said, his eyes bright with excitement. "You work for Microsoft? They are one of the greatest companies in the world."

"Well, they are good. But work there isn't always wonderful."

"I have heard of Bill Gates. He is a very smart man. You must come and see my computer school."

"I'd love to. Maybe later today, or tomorrow?"

"No. Immediately! You wait here and I will come back very soon."

He jumped up and hurried away. Minutes later, he returned on a small Honda motorcycle.

"Come with me now!" he said excitedly. "We go to my school."

"I like your motorbike," I smiled, leaving some money on the table for the waiter.

"It is not mine. I borrowed it from a friend. Let's go."

I jumped on the back of the motorcycle and soon Vu was driving me through the heavy Vietnamese traffic. Five minutes later, we were inside the computer school—one room with fifteen computers in it. Vu introduced me to Professor Than, a friendly man in his early fifties who gave private lessons in his free time.

"This is my new friend John from Microsoft," Vu told the professor. "He's going to teach me how to use Excel."

I looked down shyly. *I hope Professor Than isn't angry*, I thought. *He's Vu's teacher, not me.*

But the professor smiled, took my arm, and proudly showed me the best machine in the building.

"This is the only modern computer," he said. "None of the others have Windows 95."

I started to talk about Excel. I showed Vu how to do a simple exercise. But Vu knew how to do it better and faster than me! I tried something more difficult but, again, Vu was faster. I looked at Vu with surprise.

"You're very good at this," I said. "And, Professor Than, you teach your students very well."

"No, I'm not very smart," Vu replied. "You work for Microsoft. You're smarter than me."

After we left the computer school, Vu invited me for coffee. I was glad to accept his invitation. I wanted to learn more about this smart young man. In the café, I asked him lots of questions. Where did he go to school? Were his parents well educated? How much time did he have during the day to practice his computer studies?

"My parents are farmers," he told me. "They had no

Computers are important for Vietnam's future.

education. But they always told my younger brother and me about the importance of education. One day I hope to go to college, but now I don't have enough money. So I work six days a week, thirteen hours a day, at the hotel. I go to computer classes three evenings a week. I like working at the hotel because I can practice my English. But I know I must study hard."

"Do you have enough money for school?" I asked him. "Does the hotel pay you enough?"

"I earn $23 a month. My computer classes cost $15 a month. I give $5 to my parents because I can't help them on the farm. For food, I eat two meals a day at the hotel. When I have paid for everything, I have $3 for myself."

"Where do you sleep?"

"In a back room at the hotel. Four or five hours a day."

"Tell me more about your computer studies. How many lessons do you have each week?"

"I have enough money to practice for three hours a week at the school. But I need to do a lot more."

I thought about it for a minute, then said, "Maybe I can pay for some lessons?"

Vu looked at me seriously. "No. If you do that, you are not my friend. Let's go now."

Vu was a proud young man. I couldn't stop him paying for my coffee. But I was a proud man, too. It didn't matter what he said. *I am going to help him*, I thought.

The next morning, I asked Vu, "Do you know any bookstores that sell English books? I need more books."

Five minutes later, he was taking me to a bookstore on the back of his friend's motorcycle.

Secretly, I planned to buy Vu a lot of computer books. With these books, he could study computing skills outside the school. At the store, I found a thick, modern guide to Excel.

"This book looks really interesting," I said. "Maybe I can

22

buy it for you?"

"No. If you do that, you are not my friend!" he replied angrily. He put the book back on the shelf and took me out of the store.

How am I going to help him? I thought. I was pleased that he wanted to help himself. But I also wanted him to get a full-time education. He wasn't making it easy.

That night was my last night in Hue. I went to my favorite restaurant, a small, cheap place by the river, and ordered an ice-cold beer. Then I thought for a long time about Vu.

Suddenly, I had an idea. Maybe I could help Vu to find a scholarship? I didn't know if there were scholarship programs for students in Vietnam. But that didn't matter. *I'll give him his own private scholarship*, I thought. I quickly pulled a page out of my notebook and picked up a pen.

Dear Nguyen Thai Vu, I wrote. *My boss at Microsoft, Bill Gates, has given me money to help young computer students in Vietnam. You are a smart student, so this scholarship money is for you. Please use this money for books and practice time on computers. Microsoft and I are proud to help you. Please study hard, and please send me regular reports on your work. Good luck to you.*

Smiling to myself, I signed my name. Then I put a $20 bill into an air-mail envelope and returned to the hotel.

At the desk, Vu gave me my room key and I gave him the envelope.

"You can't open this until I'm upstairs," I told him. "And you can't talk to me about this until tomorrow morning—OK? If you are my friend, you'll promise me that."

He looked unsure, but he agreed.

Five minutes later, there was a knock on my door. There stood Vu, looking very emotional. He walked into my room with the letter in his hand. I was worried. *Maybe he's too proud to accept the scholarship money?* I thought.

"Microsoft thinks that I am a good student," he said. "So I

will study even harder and be a better student. I will send you regular reports. I am so happy. Now I will be able to spend even more time on computers."

With those words, he walked away and shut the door. I fell on my bed and cried with happiness.

Early next morning, we had our usual coffee together and he gave me a photograph of himself. Then, as we said goodbye, he said, "One day, I will be a teacher. I will help young people in my country to have a good education. You will be so proud of me."

"I promise I will return," I replied. "We will always be friends."

Since then, Vu has written me regularly with his news. He studied hard and went to college. Since his graduation, he has taught conversational French, English, and Japanese to workers for the Vietnamese National Railroad. He is married to Yen, a nurse, and has a five-year-old daughter, Thao. Thao has learned how to say "Hello, John," ready for my next visit to Hue.

Chapter 6   "Let's Think Big!"

By 2001, I was still trying to find a way of taking Books for Nepal into Vietnam. I was very busy in Nepal. I had no time to visit Vietnam. I wanted the charity to become international. But we were still only in one country.

Luckily, my problem was solved. One perfect summer afternoon, I was walking into a coffee shop on San Francisco's Fillmore Street to meet a possible donor. Suddenly my phone rang, and Erin introduced herself.

"I really want to meet you," she said. "A friend of yours, Verna, told me about your work in Nepal. I think it's wonderful. I think you can do the same in Vietnam. Can we meet?"

Two days later, we met at an Asian restaurant. As we ate, Erin talked about Vietnam.

"I spent two years there," she told me. "I ran Unilever's ice cream business. This was one of the best times of my life. I've been back in America for a few years, but I want to work in Vietnam again."

"How do you plan to do that?" I asked her.

"A company here in San Francisco has offered me a job. They buy furniture from Vietnam. But I really want to work with children. In my work for Unilever, I helped a village near our ice cream factory to build a school. That was my favorite project. Earlier this week, Verna told me about your charity. I understand that you have plans for Vietnam, but no experience of the country. I have that experience. Maybe we can work together?"

"I won't be able to pay you," I told her.

"That's all right," she replied. "I just want to do something to help Vietnamese children with their education. I'm going back to Vietnam for a friend's wedding. If you like, I can stay there longer. I can find out if your charity can work there or not."

Books for Nepal needed people like Erin, and I immediately accepted her offer. Over the next two days, I explained everything to her about the organization's business practice. Before her trip, she e-mailed friends in Vietnam and told them about Books for Nepal. She also organized meetings with members of the Vietnamese government. I was surprised and pleased with her speed of movement and the intelligence of her ideas. I knew immediately that she was perfect for my team.

Six weeks later, Erin returned to San Francisco. She was very tired from the 22-hour trip, but called immediately.

"We need to talk as soon as possible. The Vietnamese government is excited about working with us. I have a plan."

The next morning, in our favorite coffee shop, Erin gave me a book of photos. In the photo on the first page, a young Vietnamese girl was reading a book. Below it, in Erin's writing, were the words: BOOKS FOR NEPAL COMES TO VIETNAM.

I laughed. "So, uh, it's decided? That was quick."

"Well, it's your decision. But the country's ready for it. There hasn't been a war in Vietnam for ten years. Half the population is under the age of twenty. But, outside the cities, people are too poor to build good schools or libraries. And parents really want education for their children."

"I want to do this," I replied. "But there are problems. This year, we don't have more than $150,000 to spend. That's only enough to pay for our work in Nepal. Vietnam has four times as many people."

"That's right," Erin agreed. "So I'll help you to find more funds."

"But I don't have enough money to pay you."

"I've talked to a friend and my mom about this. They've offered to pay for my apartment for two months. And I have enough money in the bank for food and other things. So if you want me, you've got me for two months."

"No, I've got you for *four* months," I smiled.

"*Four* months? I don't understand."

"I'm going to give you the money for another two months. I hope $1,000 a month will be enough. In four months' time, we'll find a way to make you a full-time member of my team with a regular pay check. Until then, you have four months to bring in some serious money. So, let's get to the phones and start work!"

I was right. Erin was excellent at her job, and brought in money from donors almost every day. During one special week, she brought in $80,000—not from one big donor, but from many different ones.

We decided that now was the right time to start our first Vietnam projects. Erin flew to Vietnam, and four days later I received this e-mail:

Hi John,

I've just returned from a day in Can Gio, the poorest part of the Ho Chi Minh area. The local school is used as a primary school and middle school. It has over 500 children and is too crowded. The children only get four hours of school a day because they can't all be there at the same time. As a result, most primary-school children leave before they reach middle school. We're working with the local government to make the school bigger. We can really help these people to find a better future!

Bye from Vietnam,

Erin

I immediately started sending copies of Erin's e-mail to possible future donors for the school project in Can Gio. By the next day, I had not one donor, but two! I sent an e-mail to Erin:

Hi Erin,

Good news! I have more than one donor, so don't stop at only one school. Find other projects if you can. We can easily fund them. I know that there are only two of us, but let's think big! Good luck!

John

Erin in a Room to Read classroom in Vietnam

By late 2001, we were working in Vietnam and Nepal, with plans for Cambodia, too. We were building schools and libraries, and we were also funding computer rooms and scholarships for girls. But our organization's name was still Books for Nepal. That was a big problem for us in Vietnam. Of course, we had to change it. After a lot of thought, we decided to name our organization Room to Read.

Chapter 7   September 11

By the fall of 2001, we had teams working in Nepal and Vietnam. Money was pouring in, and we opened our 100th library. There were stories about our work in all the newspapers, and we had new fund-raising groups in New York, London, and Paris. Everything was going well.

On September 11, 2001, I was in France. A friend, Clarissa, and I were on a short cycling vacation there. She was on the phone, talking to a possible future donor in Paris. Suddenly, her face went pale. She turned off her phone and said, "We have to get to a television immediately."

We cycled quickly to a friend's house and, on his television, saw pictures of the Twin Towers on fire. One burning building, and then the other, fell to the ground. I was shocked. The world was now a very different place. I wanted to get home, immediately, to my country.

Soon after my return to San Francisco, Erin and I talked about the importance of 9/11 on our work. The future seemed very bad. *Will our project still seem important to donors?* we asked ourselves. *Maybe Americans will stop worrying about people in other countries.*

"A new group of fund-raisers in Chicago is having a meeting for possible donors in two weeks' time," Erin said. "We'll know then if Americans are still interested in our project."

Two weeks later, I was waiting nervously in a small room high above Michigan Avenue in Chicago. As I was preparing the film show for Room to Read, I was introduced to a man named Ben Shapiro.

"Don't worry," Ben said. "Everything will go well. America needs to do this kind of work now. We are the richest country on earth. We want to sell everyone Coca-Cola. Businesses like Wal-Mart use cheap workers everywhere. But we don't give other countries much in return. When the Russians left Afghanistan in 1989, Afghanistan needed new schools and hospitals urgently. America didn't build them, but America's enemies in parts of the Islamic world did. Two weeks ago, these enemies attacked us in New York and killed thousands of people. Projects like Room to Read have never been more important than now. After the meeting, I plan to give you a big check. I'm sure I won't be the only one."

I felt a lot happier after talking to Ben Shapiro. And I felt even happier after the meeting. Ben Shapiro was right. The room was full of people who were all excited about our project.

"President Bush is wrong," one woman said angrily. "He wants us to help America by going shopping. But we can change the world by helping other people. A new school in a poor country is better than a new freezer in my kitchen."

After the meeting, Room to Read had enough money for two new schools. I felt excited about our success. But I also felt proud of the American people in that room that night. Even in our worst times, Americans still wanted to help people who were halfway around the world.

◆

After 9/11, there were more checks and rules at airports. This made traveling more difficult. Two weeks after the meeting in Chicago, I was in New York's JFK Airport. I was very tired because that morning I had to be at the airport by 5:30 A.M., two hours before my flight.

The line was moving very slowly. After twenty minutes, I was at the airline desk. Next to me, a man was having a loud, angry conversation with an airline assistant.

"It's too small," he told her. "I want to take it on the plane with me."

"I'm sorry, sir, but you can't. It will have to go with the suitcases. Those are the new rules."

At first, I didn't understand what the man was talking about. He seemed to be empty-handed. He had no bags with him. Then I saw something in his hand: a small knife for opening letters.

"This letter-opener belonged to my grandfather," the man explained. "If it goes with the suitcases, it will get lost."

I decided to help him. "Excuse me, sir," I said. "I think I can solve your problem. If you give me the letter-opener and a business card, I'll put them in my suitcase. When I get to San Francisco, I'll mail it to you."

His mouth opened and he looked at me with surprise. Then he gave me the letter-opener with a business card.

"You're a complete stranger to me," he said. "But thank you."

With those words, he hurried away to join his waiting family.

"That was kind of you," the airline assistant said to me. "You're a good man."

"Maybe you can move me to a better seat?" I joked.

But the airline assistant was not amused. "Has a stranger asked you to carry anything?" she asked seriously.

"Nobody except for my new friend." I looked at his business card. "Mr. Brent Erensel," I said with a laugh.

"Sir," she said, "this is not funny. You have to be very careful when you accept packages from strangers."

"But ... but ... you heard my conversation with him. You called me a good guy for helping him!"

Without a smile, the airline assistant turned to the next

passenger.

The country was in a very, very strange state.

Two weeks later, I received a letter in the mail from my new best friend, Brent Erensel.

Dear John,

Thank you for returning my letter opener. After I received the package with your business card, I looked for Room to Read on the Internet. The children in the photos look so happy. I've decided that you and Erin are very special people. I've put a little check in with this letter for your charity.

With warmest thoughts,

Brent

With the letter was a check for $1,000. I was grateful, but I was also surprised. When I helped him at the airport, I wasn't looking for donations. But because of this help, Room to Read now had half the money that it needed for a new school library.

Brent's donation and the success of the meeting in Chicago were important signs of hope. Their message was clear. Even after 9/11, people, more than ever, wanted to do good things for the world. Room to Read must continue to grow.

Chapter 8 "Your Life is a Mess."

By 2003, our team of fund-raising volunteers was working like a well-oiled machine. From Seattle to London, from Hong Kong to New York, there were hundreds of people raising money for Room to Read. In the spring of 2002, one of our volunteers even held a fund-raising party in a big tent on Mount Everest!

Room to Read was fast becoming a big international organization, but it didn't have many full-time, paid organizers. As a result, I had to do the work of many people. I ran a large, international charity, but I was its director of fund-raising, too.

I had to make plans, employ new people, and put money in the bank. But I also answered telephones, put stamps on envelopes, and even cleaned the office.

Because Erin and I did the work of many people, there was more money for schools, libraries, and scholarships. The long hours didn't worry us. We felt lucky because we loved our work. But there was a high personal price to pay for all our success.

I didn't see my family very often, and I almost never had a vacation. Most importantly, I had no time for serious romance. Girlfriends soon got bored with me because I spent too much time on my work. One woman told me, "Room to Read is your wife, your lover, your child, your family dog, and your job."

When I agreed with her, she was not happy.

"That's not the right answer," she said.

"I'm sorry," I replied. "But Room to Read means everything to me. Every morning, I jump out of bed with a big smile on my face, happy to go to the office. I feel lucky because I love my work so much."

I wasn't the best person in the world to have as a boyfriend!

♦

On a warm, spring day in 2003, I was late for a meeting in my office with two possible donors. I drove too fast and was stopped by a policeman. As he was getting off his motorcycle, notebook in hand, I opened the window.

"How are you?" I smiled at him weakly.

"I'm fine," he replied. "But I'm worried about your speed. Can I see your driving papers?"

The police officer watched impatiently as I searched through the mess in my car. I finally found them in a pile of urgent phone messages which still waiting for my reply. The officer wasn't amused. He looked through my papers carefully.

"These papers say that you live in Washington State. You

need new ones for California."

"I know," I replied with a shy, nervous smile. "I have the forms in my bag. I'm sorry, but I've been very busy …"

"Can I see them, please?"

I went to the back of the car for my bag. The back was a mess, too—boxes of children's books, piles of papers, tennis balls, running shoes, and dirty clothes everywhere. I finally found the bag, opened it, and showed him the forms. He studied them carefully, and returned them to me with a sad shake of his head.

"Your life is a mess," he said.

I thought of all the other disorganization in my private life—the old, smelly food in my refrigerator, the unpaid bills on my desk …

"Yes, sir, it is," I had to agree. "I'm sorry."

"I won't punish you this time," the officer finally said.

"Really? Do you mean that?" I smiled. "Thank you!"

I must send those forms off today, I thought. But in my heart I knew that this was impossible. There were other, more urgent, things for me to do. I had to raise money for Room to Read.

♦

While we were raising plenty of money for the charity, my personal position wasn't so good. By early 2003, I was in my third year of life without a regular pay check. I had little money now from my days as a well-paid sales director at Microsoft.

I tried to forget about my money problems. I had more important things to think about. But one Sunday afternoon in San Francisco, I realized the true size of my problem. I was running through the city when I noticed a FOR SALE sign outside a beautiful house.

I want that house, I thought. I went inside and looked around. It was exactly what I wanted. But then I saw the price. *Oh, no,*

I thought. *That's too expensive.*

I left the house immediately and walked sadly back to my apartment. Later that night, I had dinner with my friend Laura.

"I'm almost 40," I said. "But I don't even have enough money to buy my own home here in San Francisco. What kind of success is this?" I talked for a long time about my unhappiness at not having money. Laura listened to me patiently. The next morning, she sent me an e-mail.

John,

This is not the right time for you to own a beautiful house. Think about schools and libraries for the poor people of this world, not houses for yourself. Their need is greater than yours. You're a lucky man, John. You're doing exactly what you want to do with your life. Not many people can say that.

I knew that she was right. I felt sorry about my silly, selfish thoughts of the day before. I still had lessons to learn.

Chapter 9   Cambodia

By this time, Room to Read was also helping children in Cambodia. Some people were worried that we were growing too quickly. But luckily, many volunteers were helping to find donors for us.

One school donor in Nepal, Hilary Valentine, decided to become a fund-raiser for us. On a Friday evening early in 2003, she organized a big fund-raising meeting at the Alpine Hills Tennis Club in California. At the meeting, I showed films of our projects, and talked about our Room to Grow girls' scholarship program in Nepal and Vietnam. Then I talked about Cambodia.

"Many girls there have no families. Their parents were killed by the Khmer Rouge. We want these girls to have

Some of the first scholarship girls in Nepal

a good education and a better start in life. We would like to give one hundred scholarships immediately. But we don't have the funds. We need the money before the school year starts in three months' time. With your help, we can give these girls the life-changing gift of education."

"How much do you need?" asked a loud voice from the back of the room.

The voice belonged to Don Listwin, a well-known, rich California businessman and donor of much money to educational and health charities.

"Each scholarship will cost $250 a year. So for a hundred girls, we need $25,000 a year."

Don stood up and talked to the other people at the meeting. "For every school and scholarship that you fund," he told them, "I will fund one, too."

In less than two minutes, he raised more than $150,000 for our Cambodia program! It was the most successful meeting in our young history.

But this wasn't the only happy ending. In June 2005, Hilary Valentine and Don Listwin got married. As a wedding gift, I personally funded a girl's scholarship. I didn't—this time—ask Don to fund one, too!

♦

History hasn't been kind to the people of Cambodia. By the early 1990s, after years of wars and the murder of millions of people by the Khmer Rouge, the country had no money, no organization, millions of children without parents, and no government. On my first trip to the country in the early 1990s, I was sad to see so much pain and unhappiness. But I quickly fell in love with its people. They have suffered terribly, but they still get up before the sun every morning for a long day's work in their rice fields or small businesses, or for school.

By the spring of 2003, Room to Read had a small team of local people working in an office in Phnom Penh. Soon after our successful fund-raising meeting in California, I visited Cambodia to see our first projects in the company of the new team.

My first few days were spent quietly in Phnom Penh, riding around the city on the back of a small motorcycle, with a different driver every day. One morning, I asked my driver about his life.

"What are your dreams for the future?" I asked him.

"Before 1995, I spoke no English," he replied. "But now, every day, I learn. I have two young sons. Every day, I tell them to study and learn more than me. I was young during the time of the Khmer Rouge. I have almost no education. But my sons will have a better life than me. If they study hard, maybe one day they will work for the government or in the office of a business."

Arriving at the Java coffeehouse, I wanted to give the driver money for his sons' education. But then I remembered my experience with my friend Vu in Vietnam, and I gave him only

$2, double the usual cost of a ride.

"Your sons are lucky to have a good father like you," I told him.

The next morning, I left Phnom Penh with Dim Boramy, our country director, for the long three-hour drive to the Tong Slek Secondary School in the north-east of the country. Twelve teachers and a few hundred students were waiting for me to open the first school computer room in this part of the country.

As the head teacher showed me around the new computer room, I noticed a bed in the corner. Boramy asked the teachers about this. A dark-haired teacher in his late twenties explained.

"The computer room has no lock on the door or window. Until the room is safe from thieves, a different teacher sleeps here every night."

As I was making a note of this in my notebook, a small boy stood in front of me.

"Thank you for Room to Read," he said in perfect English. "My dream is to be a businessman." With those words, he gave me a drawing.

"Thank you," I replied. "Can I keep the drawing?"

"Yes," he said, and shook my hand like a serious businessman.

After this, we all went outside into the schoolyard, to hear the head teacher's speech. The yard was crowded with hundreds of children, some of them Room to Read scholarship girls. The head teacher began by welcoming the important people from the village and our team to the Tong Slek School. Then, looking at me, he said,

"Please tell your donors that we are very happy today. Now our students don't have to leave our village to have a good education. If they stay until grade nine, they will learn English and computers. That will give them a better future. Thank you."

A female teacher then stood up. The head teacher looked surprised because women in country areas don't usually speak in front of a lot of people.

"My dream is to be a businessman."

"In our country, education for girls is not thought to be very important. But Room to Read has helped female teachers like me to understand computers. You did not just teach the male teachers. And you say that this new computer room is for all children, not only boys. It is going to change the lives of all the girls living in this area. I have only one request for you, Mr. John. The teacher from Room to Read is good and helpful, but we haven't learned enough from him yet. Can he stay for one more month?"

The teacher was a smart, nineteen-year-old student from a computer college in the city.

"Would you like to stay here for another month?" I asked him.

"Yes, please," he answered excitedly.

38

I turned quietly to Boramy. "How much are we paying him?" I asked.

"Twenty-five dollars a month," was the reply.

I turned back to the female teacher. "Mr. Boramy is the country director," I told her. "Only he can decide."

Boramy was trying to look serious, but there was already a big smile on his face.

"Yes, yes," he said twice, once in Khmer, once in English.

The teachers looked pleased, but no one was happier than me. As I saw the teachers' smiling faces and the look of excitement in the children's eyes, I was sure of one thing. I was right to bring Room to Read to Cambodia.

I made a short speech and opened the computer room. Then I wanted to learn more about our scholarship girls. The head teacher introduced me to Nam Sreyny. A shy sixteen-year-old, she told me about her early education.

"My family has money problems," she told me. "My father

Cambodian students at the opening of their new computer room

died two years ago. He was a soldier. The government didn't give us any help. My mother and I work on a small farm. Life is very hard. My mother has no money to send me to school. I had to leave school after grade six."

Luckily, Room to Read already knew about Nam's problems from the village teachers. The local team offered her a scholarship. The money paid for her school clothes and equipment. It also paid one of the teachers to give her a room and meals during the week. And it even paid for a bicycle. So, on weekends, Nam can go home to help her mother on the farm.

Chapter 10   After the Tsunami

We had a very busy, successful year in 2004. We opened Room to Read in India, and my travels took me to Cambodia, Singapore, Hong Kong, London, and Ethiopia. Room to Read was five years old and, in those five years, I almost never had time for a vacation. So, when Christmas came, I decided I needed a quiet, one-week rest away from e-mails and televisions.

I spent three days with friends at their beach house in San Diego. I went running and bicycling along the beach. I sat in bright sunshine at a beach café, listening to Christmas songs—a strange but enjoyable experience. After San Diego, I went to my sister's house in Colorado. Then I received a worrying phone message from a friend:

Turn on the news immediately. A big tsunami has hit Asia.

I turned on the television and saw terrible pictures from Indonesia, Thailand, Sri Lanka, and other countries around the Indian Ocean. Thousands of people were already dead. Towns, farms, villages, roads, hospitals and schools were destroyed. Thousands of children were without parents.

Who is going to help these poor children? I thought.

I picked up my phone and booked an immediate flight home to San Francisco.

My vacation was at an end.

The next day, December 29, I arrived back at my San Francisco office. Only a few people were there, receiving the usual end-of-year donations. They seemed surprised to see me.

"The people in the tsunami-hit areas need money immediately to rebuild their schools," I said. "I must e-mail a few friends for money."

I sat down at my computer. But before I could send my first e-mail, I received a message from my friend Bob Uppington. He ran an educational charity in Sri Lanka. The news from there was even more shocking than I thought.

More than 200 villages have lost their schools, he wrote. *Tomorrow we're planning to take food, water, and medicines to the east coast of the country.*

I sent him an immediate reply:

We will help villages that have lost their schools. I promise that we will find them money for new schools as soon as possible.

Our small team spent all night e-mailing and calling possible donors. Early the next morning, I received a call from Michele. She worked for us, giving information to newspapers, and to TV and radio stations, about our work.

"Good news!" she said. "You are going to talk on CNN about rebuilding schools in Sri Lanka."

"But I've never been to Sri Lanka," I said. "I don't know the names of any Sri Lankan villages. And we don't have any clear plans yet ..."

"Don't worry," Michele said calmly. "You have a lot of experience in Asia. You worked there for Microsoft for five years. Room to Read has built more libraries there than any other charity. On television, you can tell millions of people about the great work your team is doing."

On the evening of January 1, a bored-looking cameraman showed me to my seat in front of a large photo of San Francisco by night. I wasn't facing an interviewer—I was sitting opposite a wall!

"Where's the person who's going to interview me?" I asked the cameraman.

"You won't see her," the cameraman explained. "She's going to talk to you from Atlanta. Put this in your ear. You'll hear all the questions through this. The interview will start in three minutes."

Three minutes later, I was on national television. I looked at the wall in front of me and answered questions about Room to Read and its plans for Sri Lanka. The four minutes of the interview went very quickly.

Then, my phone rang. It was a friend from Seattle.

"I've just seen you on CNN," he said. "You were good, but your tie was terrible!"

My phone continued to ring all night and for many weeks after that. Many CNN viewers wanted to help. High school students, old friends—all of them had great ideas for raising funds for schools in Sri Lanka.

♦

By now, I wanted the world to know about Room to Read. On January 10, 2005, I started a round-the-world trip with stops in Hong Kong, Singapore, Zurich, and London.

In Hong Kong, I did three newspaper, one magazine, and two television interviews. Between these, I took a call from a rich family that offered a donation of $50,000 for rebuilding projects in Sri Lanka. At a breakfast meeting, a Hong Kong company gave us another $100,000.

In Singapore, I did many more interviews. One of them was with Suba Sivakumaran, a reporter who was born in Sri Lanka. I answered her questions about my plans for Sri Lanka, and she became more and more interested. Finally, she said, "I'm

42

planning to take time off work. I want to go back to Sri Lanka as a volunteer."

Suddenly, *I* was interviewing *her*! We needed good people in Sri Lanka, and she seemed perfect. I told Erin about Suba. Erin spoke to her on the phone and, one week later, Suba was our new country director for Room to Read in Sri Lanka.

Room to Read received hundreds more offers of help after the television interviews. Schools from Malaysia to Tokyo to Vancouver to London started fund-raising projects. Scholastic, the biggest children's book company in the world, offered us half a million books. They even volunteered to pay for the cost of sending them.

In April, Erin left for her first visit to Sri Lanka. There, she was excited to meet Suba for the first time. She was also excited to visit Room to Read's new projects—more than twelve of them already!

During Erin's visit to Sri Lanka, I went to a meeting at Oxford University in England. A few days later, I woke up and turned on my computer. My first e-mail message was from Erin:

Subject: A Message of Hope from Sri Lanka

Dear Room to Read Family and Friends,

I have just returned from an emotional trip to Ampara, on the east coast of Sri Lanka. It took us more than nine hours by car, traveling through the mountains over narrow, crowded, badly-built roads.

Before I visited the school projects, I toured the tsunami-hit area. The suffering here is terrible. About 12,000 people died in Ampara on that quiet Sunday morning when the big waves came. In some areas buildings are completely destroyed. In other areas, only pieces of wall show the places where houses stood. Again and again I hear heart-breaking stories from the local people. One man lost all six of his children and his wife. One child lost both parents and his four brothers and sisters. Everyone has lost someone who they loved.

There are tents everywhere. Luckily, there is enough clean water and food. But people are angry. It is almost four months since the tsunami, but they still haven't received much help from the government or charities. The local people are trying to clear their broken homes from the land by hand. Women are doing most of the work. The men point out at the ocean and ask about their new fishing boats. "Donors have given lots of money," they say. "So where are our boats?"

But there is some good news. We met with Shiva Charity. With their help, we are rebuilding schools in the area destroyed by the tsunami. Two teams are working full-time, rebuilding more than twenty schools. We are one of the first organizations to begin rebuilding projects here. Three schools are already finished. Each school has about fifty children, and is also used as a meeting place for women.

This country already has a special place in my heart. I am so proud of our work here.

All the best to you all,

Erin

In another e-mail to me personally, Erin wrote,

I don't think twenty schools are enough. Suba and I agree that we

A Sri Lankan student in his new school after the tsunami

need double that number. Can we do that?

As usual, and without having the funds, I answered yes. There were more than one hundred messages waiting in my in-box. Most of them had subject lines like "How can I help?"

Later that day, a group of Oxford students gave me a check for $16,000. That was enough money for one more school already!

Luckily, funds continued arriving regularly. One year after the tsunami, twenty-two new schools in Ampara were open, and another sixteen were almost ready. Not happy with that, Suba and her team were planning to build sixty more schools over the next two years.

Our success in Sri Lanka teaches us all a very important lesson, I think. When you need to do something quickly and urgently, don't think too deeply about the problems. Act immediately! If you believe in your dream enough, others will believe in it, too. And you will succeed.

Chapter 11   The Millionth Book

It was November 2005, and I was flying from Bangkok to Kathmandu, thinking about the trip to Bahundanda with my father six and a half years earlier.

Room to Read was now working in six countries. Six and a half years earlier, there were only two people in the team— Dinesh Shrestha and me. Now there were fifty full-time, paid workers and more than 1,000 volunteer fund-raisers. We now had more than 2,300 libraries, and this week was a special week for us. Room to Read was donating its one millionth book.

Celebrations were organized by Dinesh—three activity-filled days of meetings with head teachers, conversations with village governments, visits to twenty-one schools, and, on my last day in the country, the celebration of the millionth book at the opening of a new library.

Outside the busy airport, I saw Dinesh waiting for me in the crowd. I waved at him and shouted, "Bai!"—Nepali for "younger brother." He happily shook my hand and welcomed me back to Nepal.

As we were driving through the busy streets of Kathmandu, he said, "This Friday will be a big day."

"I know that," I said with surprise. "That's why I'm here."

He laughed. "Are you excited about it?"

"Of course," I replied, even more surprised. "Dinesh, why are you laughing?"

"Because we are not going to open only one library on Friday," he said. "We wanted to make the day special. So on Friday between 10:00 A.M. and midday, we will celebrate the opening of thirty new libraries across Nepal."

I was shocked. But I was also proud of Dinesh and his team for their adventurous plans.

After two busy but enjoyable days of visiting new schools, speaking to head teachers, and meeting crowds of excited children, the day of the millionth book finally arrived.

I woke at 7:30 and I walked the streets of Kathmandu for an hour. I loved the city at this time of day. There was little traffic, and the early morning air was clean and fresh.

Back at the Kathmandu Guest House, I had a large pot of milk tea with Dinesh and Rajeev, the director of our library program. Everybody was smiling, as excited about the day as I was. Then Dinesh gave me some very surprising news.

"Today, all across Nepal, 123 new libraries will open!"

We had to be at the opening of three libraries in the Kathmandu Valley, so I quickly paid our bill. On the way to our car, I smiled at Rajeev.

"In the early days," I told him, "Dinesh and I hoped to open 123 new libraries in our lifetime. We never imagined 123 libraries opening in one day!"

An hour's drive from our guesthouse, Dinesh parked his small car (no big cars for our low-cost organization!) next to a field and we walked the last hundred meters to the school. We were met by a small crowd of teachers offering the warmest welcomes and greetings. The students formed two lines. As we walked between them, they put flowers around our necks. I tried to stop and say thank you to each student. Some smiled and said, "You're welcome, sir." Others looked shyly at the ground.

We were shown to seats that were thoughtfully placed on a small stage out of the sun. In front of us, students were sitting down in the school's yard on long, wooden seats.

At the small microphone near the front of the stage, the head teacher made a short speech.

"This is one of the biggest days in the history of the school …" he began.

Next, a group of girl students did a dance and sang,

John and Dinesh at the opening of a new library in Nepal

"Now we have a Room to Read.

"We will study every day.

"We will learn Nepali and English.

"We will speak them perfectly."

A few teachers and a member of the village government then spoke. As they talked to the crowd of students and parents about the importance of reading and their goals for the future, I was thinking about other parts of Nepal. In my imagination, I was high in the sky above the country, looking down on 123 villages. In the shadows of the Himalayas, in villages on the sides of steep, green hills, in narrow river valleys, and in the city of Kathmandu, similar crowds of students, teachers, and parents were celebrating the opening of Room to Read libraries. *From today,* I thought, *37,000 children will be able to do something that their parents could never do. They will be able to borrow books in different languages—a very important part of every child's education.*

In my imagination, I went higher above the earth and looked down on India, Laos, Sri Lanka, Cambodia, and Vietnam. I thought about all the other Room to Read projects that, with the help of local people and hundreds of volunteers, now existed in those countries: 2,300 libraries; more than 200 schools; 50 computer and language rooms; 1,700 girls with scholarships; a million books.

The head teacher said something to me, and I fell quickly back to earth. It was time for me to open the new library. I cut the long, thin piece of shiny red cloth that was hanging across the door. The air was filled with noisy celebrations. Dinesh and I walked into a brightly-painted room full of desks, chairs, and shelves of books in Nepali and English.

That day, the two of us stopped work to celebrate. But there was more work waiting for us the next day. There were thousands more libraries for us to open in the future. Millions of kids were waiting for a better future. I didn't want them to wait too long.

The Latest News

Room to Read has continued to grow and by 2010 there were more than 10,000 girls in the Girls' Education program. There were 1,000 schools and 10,000 libraries, and more than eight million new books in school libraries, half of them in the students' own languages. There were plans for Tanzania to become the tenth Room to Read country.

John continues to travel the world to raise funds for Room to Read. He has also written his first children's book, *Zak the Yak with Books on His Back*. *Leaving Microsoft to Change the World* can now be read in twenty different languages. For more news about Room to Read's work, visit www.roomtoread.org.

ACTIVITIES

Chapters 1–2

Before you read

1 Look at the Word List at the back of the book. Which words are

    a for people?

    b about learning?

    c about giving money and helping people?

2 Discuss these questions with another student.

    a Have you ever given money to

      • a member of your family?

      • a friend?

      • a poor person on the street?

      • a local charity?

      • an international charity?

      Why (not)?

    b How many big international charities can you think of? In your opinion, which are the most / least important? Why?

    c What do you know about Nepal? Find information about the country in books or on the Internet. Would you like to go there on vacation? Why (not)?

While you read

3 Are these sentences right (✓) or wrong (✗)?

    a John Wood often went on long vacations. ......

    b The Nepalese are interested in education. ......

    c The school in Bahundanda was hot and crowded. ......

    d John asked his friends to send books to Nepal. ......

    e More women than men in the world cannot read. ......

    f Dinesh Shrestha was an old friend of John's father. ......

    g John wanted his father to go with him to Nepal. ......

    h The books arrived in Bahundanda on the backs of animals. ......

4 How were these people important in this part of John's story?

    a Pasupathi   **b** a head teacher in Bahundanda

    c John's father   **d** Andrew Carnegie

    e Dinesh Shrestha **f** John's friends

5 Discuss how these people felt, and why.

    a John, when he was talking to Pasupathi

    b Pasupathi, about his job

    c children of Bahundanda, when they first saw John

    d John, when he was talking to the head teacher of the school

    e John, after his visit to Colorado, when he received his father's e-mail

    f John, about his new job in Beijing

    g Sushil, when he met John

6 Work with another student. Have this conversation between John and his father.

    Student A: You are John's father. You really want to go to Nepal. Tell your son why.

    Student B: You are John. You don't want to go to Nepal with your father. Tell him why, but don't hurt his feelings.

Chapters 3–4

Before you read

7 How did John feel when he returned to Beijing after his trip to Bahundanda? Why? What do you think?

While you read

8 What did John do first? Number these in the right order, 1–8.

    a He met Bill Draper.   ......

    b He told Mike about leaving Microsoft.   ......

    c He told Sophie about his plan to leave Microsoft.   ......

    d He decided to follow his dream.   ......

    e He started Books for Nepal.   ......

    f He organized Bill Gates's visit to China.   ......

    g He met the DRF fund director.   ......

    h He asked unsuccessfully for money.   ......

9 Discuss whose words these were. Who were they talking or writing to? What did they mean?

a "How are we going to live?"

b "Different things have become important to you now."

c "I need you here."

d "I'm leaving everything behind me."

e "The head teachers of the two schools would like you to visit this fall."

f "I'll discuss your project with other people."

g "My goal is for anyone—from rich bankers to ordinary school teachers—to help us."

h "I will enjoy working with you."

10 Work with another student. Have this conversation between John and Sophie.

Student A: You are John, in Beijing. Tell Sophie about your plans.

Student B: You are Sophie. You don't like John's plans. Tell him why.

11 Discuss these questions with another student. What do you think?

a Was Michael right to be angry with John? Why (not)?

b Do you feel sorry for Sophie? Why (not)?

Chapters 5–6

Before you read

12 What do you know about Vietnam? What problems has the country had over the last 60 years? Find information in books or on the Internet, and discuss it with another student.

While you read

13 Underline the right words.

a In 1997, John was in Hue on *business / vacation*.

b Vu *liked / didn't like* working in a hotel.

c Vu *asked / didn't ask* John for money.

d John *bought / didn't buy* Vu a guide to Excel.

e Vu *accepted / didn't accept* "scholarship" money from John.

f Vu later worked as a *farmer / teacher.*

g When she met John, Erin *already knew / didn't know* Vietnam.

h John gave Erin money for *two / four months'* work.

i Erin's main job was looking for *donors / volunteers.*

j By late 2001, Books for Nepal was working in *two / three* countries.

After you read

14 Discuss who these words describe.

    a proud and impatient   **b** kind and friendly

    c emotional and grateful   **d** fast and organized

15 How were these important in this part of John's story?

    a a bookstore   **b** Bill Gates

    c a railroad company   **d** a friend called Verna

    e a wedding   **f** Erin's mother and friend

    g Can Gio   **h** a change of name

16 Discuss these statements with another student. Do you agree with them? Why (not)?

    a "Computers and English are both important for everyone's future."

    b "It is wrong to accept money from a friend."

    c "John was a bad employer because he didn't pay his workers enough money."

Chapters 7–9

Before you read

17 What problems did Room to Read have after September 11, 2001? Why? What do you think?

While you read

18 Write the missing word.

    a By the fall of 2001, Room to Read was opening its 100th ....

    b President Bush wanted people to help America by going ....

    c One man couldn't take a .... on a plane.

    d John had no time for serious ....

e One spring day in 2003, John was stopped by a

....

f John was sad because he couldn't buy

a ....

g At a big fund-raising meeting in California, John raised

money for .... for girls in Cambodia.

h At the Tong Slek Secondary School, a teacher slept in the

.... room.

i In country areas in Cambodia, ... didn't

usually speak in front of a lot of people.

j Room to Read paid for Nam Sreyny's school clothes,

equipment, room, meals, and a ....

After you read

19 Match the first halves of the sentences in A with the correct
second halves in B.

A

a After 9/11, John felt ......

b After the meeting in Chicago, John felt ......

c After his conversation with John at the airport,
Bret Erensel felt ......

d John worked long hours but he felt ......

e After he stopped John, the police officer felt ......

f After John visited a house for sale, he felt ......

g After he received Laura's e-mail, John felt ......

h After the big California meeting, Don Listwin felt ......

i At the Tong Slek Secondary School, the head teacher
felt ......

j Nam Sreyny felt ......

B

1) proud of Americans.

2) sorry about his earlier thoughts.

3) lucky.

4) sorry for himself.

5) happy and in love.

6) worried about the future.

54

7) worried about the computer room.

8) happier about her life.

9) impatient and not amused.

10) surprised and grateful.

20 Look at your answers to Question 19. Discuss why those people felt that way.

21 Work with another student. Have this conversation between John and a friend.

Student A: You are John. Tell your friend about the problems in your personal life. Reply to your friend's suggestions.

Student B: You are the friend. What can John do to make his personal life better? Make suggestions

Chapters 10–11

Before you read

22 Find information about the big tsunami in December 2004. Which countries were worst hit? What problems did people in those countries have after the tsunami?

While you read

23 Underline the wrong words and write the correct ones.

a John heard bad news while he was on vacation at his parents' home. ....

b John was taken to a TV center in Atlanta. ....

c During his round-the-world trip, John visited Hong Kong, Singapore, Tokyo, and London. ....

d Suba Sivakumaran met Erin before she became the Room to Read country director in Sri Lanka. ....

e Erin visited Sri Lanka four weeks after the tsunami. ....

f John was at the opening of three new schools in the Kathmandu Valley. ....

g Room to Read started work in South Africa in 2006, South America in 2007, and Bangladesh in 2008. ....

After you read

24 How did John feel, and why

    a   in a beach café in San Diego?

    b   when he watched television in Colorado?

    c   after Bob Uppington's e-mail?

    d   when a cameraman showed him to his seat?

    e   after the CNN interview?

    f   after his interview with Suba Sivakumaran?

    g   after Dinesh told him about the plans for Friday?

    h   during the speeches at the Shree Ram Janaki School?

25 John says, "When you need to do something quickly and urgently, don't think too deeply about the problems. Act immediately!" Do you agree with him? Why (not)? Discuss your opinions.

Writing

26 Imagine that you are John and you have just finished your vacation in Nepal (Chapter 1). Write about the trip in your notebook. How do you feel? Why? How will this vacation be important to you in the future?

27 You are John (Chapter 3). Write a letter to your father. Tell him about your plans to leave Microsoft. Why do you want to leave? What problems will there be for you in the future? How do you feel about them now?

28 You are Sophie (Chapter 3). Write a letter to John. You think that he is making a big mistake. Tell him why.

29 You are John (Chapter 4). Write your business plan for Bill Draper. How do you plan to raise funds? Who is going to help you, and why? How are local people in Nepal going to help? Why do you need money from DRF?

30 You are Vu (Chapter 5). Write a letter to John. Tell him about your life since you graduated from college.

31 John has a strange, amusing experience at an airport in Chapter 7. Write about something strange or amusing that has happened to *you* at an airport or railroad station.

32 Choose three of these people. How are they important to Room to Read? Write a few lines about each of them.

a Dinesh Shrestha   **b** Erin   **c** Vu   **d** Suba Sivakumaran

33 You are a reporter at the opening of the Shree Ram Janaki School (Chapter 11). Interview John Wood. Ask him about his feelings and his plans for the future. Write a description of the celebrations and your interview with John Wood for your newspaper.

34 You are a fund-raiser for Room to Read. Write a full-page report for your local newspaper about Room to Read. Choose good pictures from the Internet for your report. Write a short, interesting description of Room to Read's work. Say why you need money *now*!

35 You would like to work for Room to Read in Nepal, Vietnam, or Cambodia. Write a letter to John. Why do you want to work for Room to Read? What personal and professional skills can you bring? Which country would you like to work in? Why?

WORD LIST

celebrate (v) to do something special because something good has happened

charity (n) an organization that gives money or other help to poor people or people in trouble

director (n) the top person in an organization or business

donate (v) to give money, food, clothes, or other things to charity. A **donor** is a person who donates.

educate (v) to teach at school, college, or university

emotional (adj) with strong feelings. You feel very sad, happy, or proud, for example.

experience (n/v) skill or understanding that you get from a job, an activity, or from life

funds (n) the money that you need for something. When you **fund** a special activity, you give the money for it.

member (n) someone who has joined a club, group, or organization

primary school (n) school for children between the ages of about five and eleven

project (n) important work that is planned carefully over a long time

raise (funds) (v) to find the money for a special activity by asking for a lot of people's help

run (v) to organize a business, an organization, or an activity

scholarship (n) money that is given to someone for their education

secondary school (n) school for children between the ages of about eleven and eighteen

shock (n/v) a very great surprise, often a bad one

tsunami (n) a great and sudden movement of the waves in the ocean

village (n) a group of houses, stores, and businesses in country areas, smaller than a town

volunteer (n/v) someone who offers to work for no money

yak (n) a long-haired, four-legged animal that lives in high areas of Asia